Mother
Vertis
Osby

Trust In the Lord

Written and compiled
by Sarah M. Hupp

Illustrated by C. James Frazier

Designed by Arlene Greco

INSPIRE

Inspire Books is an imprint
of Peter Pauper Press, Inc.

For permissions please see the
last page of this book.

Text copyright © 1999
Peter Pauper Press, Inc.
202 Mamaroneck Avenue
White Plains, NY 10601
Illustrations copyright © C. James Frazier,
Licensed by Wild Apple Licensing
All rights reserved
ISBN 0-88088-131-3
Printed in China
7 6 5 4 3 2 1

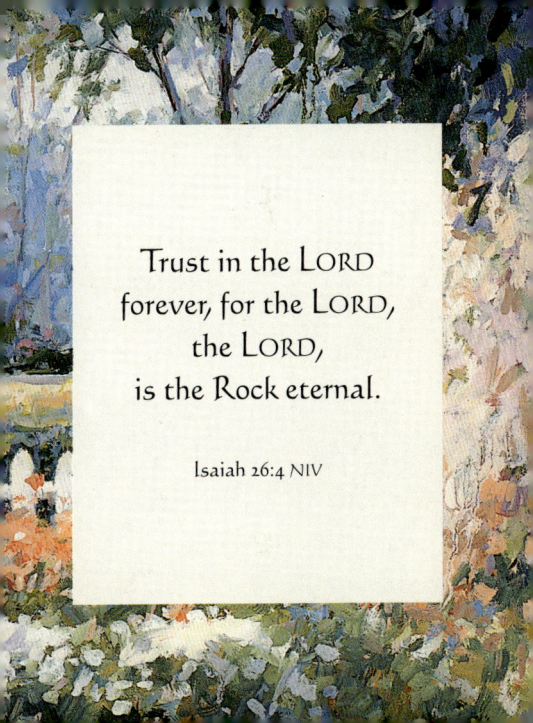

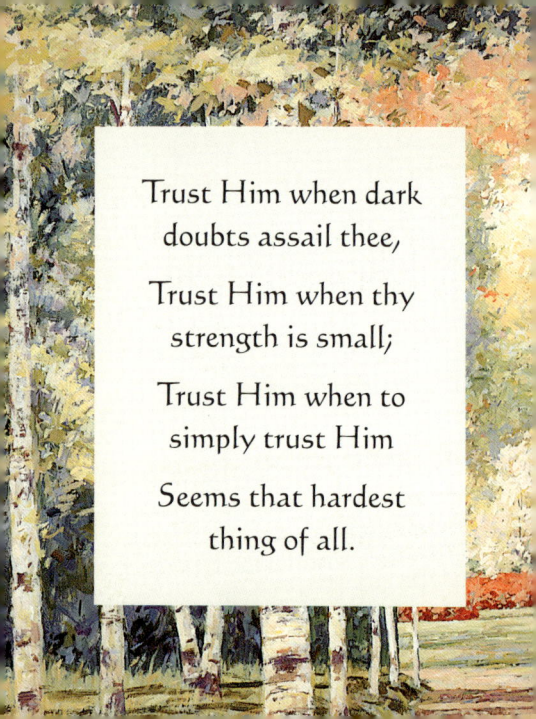

Trust Him when dark doubts assail thee,

Trust Him when thy strength is small;

Trust Him when to simply trust Him

Seems that hardest thing of all.

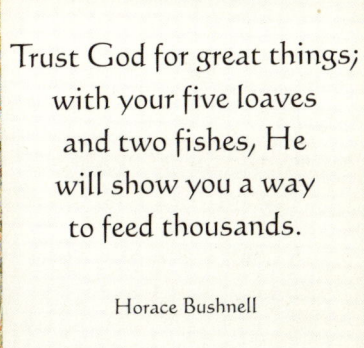

Trust God for great things; with your five loaves and two fishes, He will show you a way to feed thousands.

Horace Bushnell

For in Scripture it says: "See, I lay a stone in Zion, a chosen and precious cornerstone, and the one who trusts in him will never be put to shame."

1 Peter 2:6 NIV

There is no room for the word *disappointment* in the happy life of entire trust in Jesus and satisfaction with His perfect and glorious will.

Frances Ridley Havergal

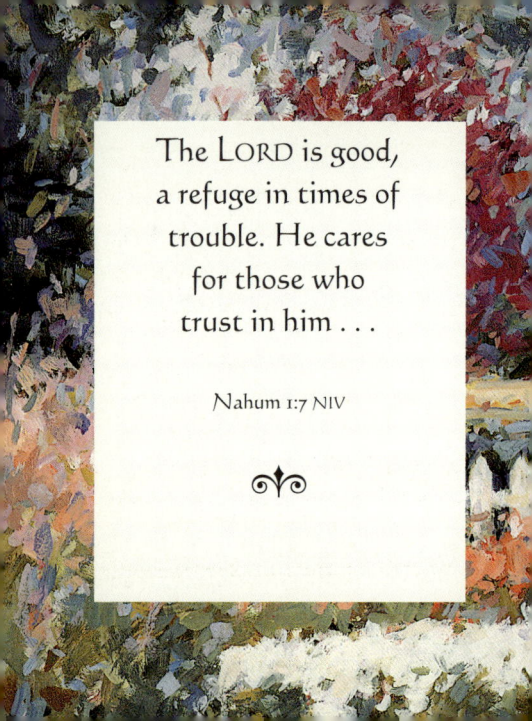

The LORD is good,
a refuge in times of
trouble. He cares
for those who
trust in him . . .

Nahum 1:7 NIV

God can summon unexpected reinforcements at any moment to help His people. Believe that He is between you and your difficulty, and what troubles you will flee before Him, as clouds in the wind.

F. B. Meyer

Trust in him at all times,
O people; pour out
your hearts to him, for
God is our refuge.

Psalm 62:8 NIV

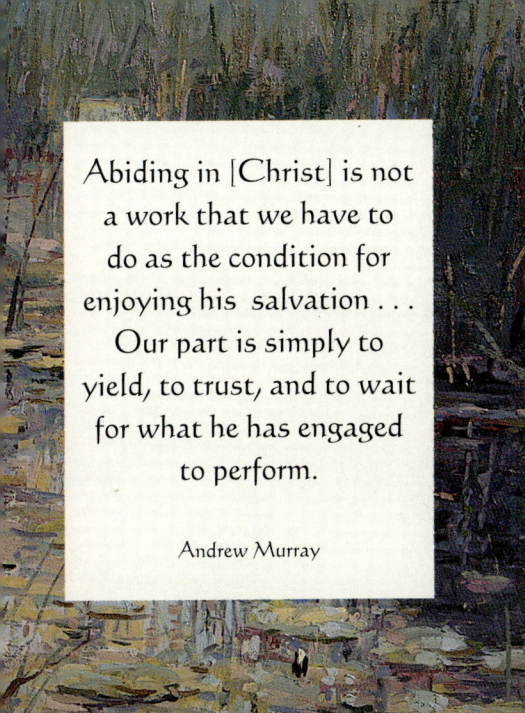

Abiding in [Christ] is not a work that we have to do as the condition for enjoying his salvation... Our part is simply to yield, to trust, and to wait for what he has engaged to perform.

Andrew Murray

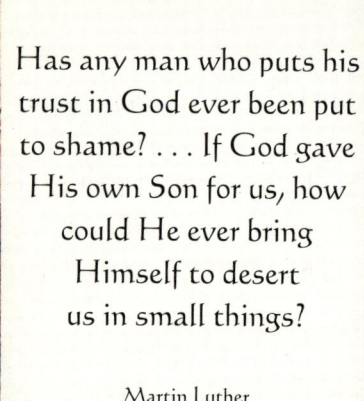

Has any man who puts his trust in God ever been put to shame? . . . If God gave His own Son for us, how could He ever bring Himself to desert us in small things?

Martin Luther

Trust in the LORD with all your heart, and do not lean on your own understanding. In all your ways acknowledge Him, and He will make your paths straight.

Proverbs 3:5–6 NASB

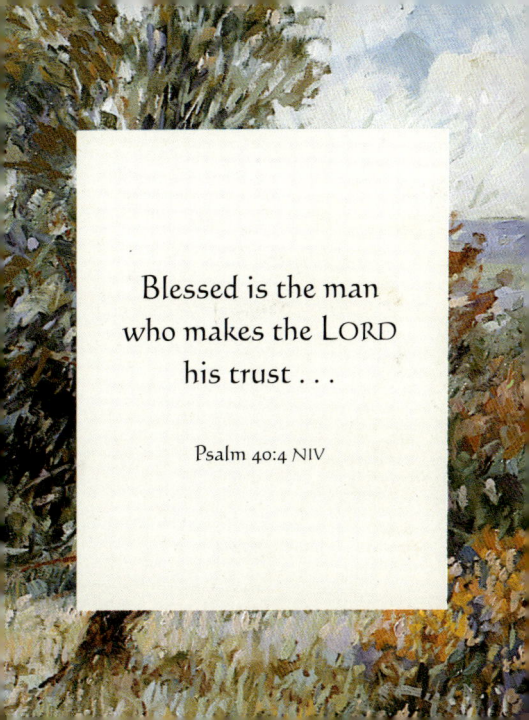

Blessed is the man
who makes the LORD
his trust . . .

Psalm 40:4 NIV

Yield to the Lord with simple heart,
All that thou hast, and all thou art;
Renounce all strength but strength Divine,
And peace shall be for ever thine . . .

Madame Jeanne Guyon

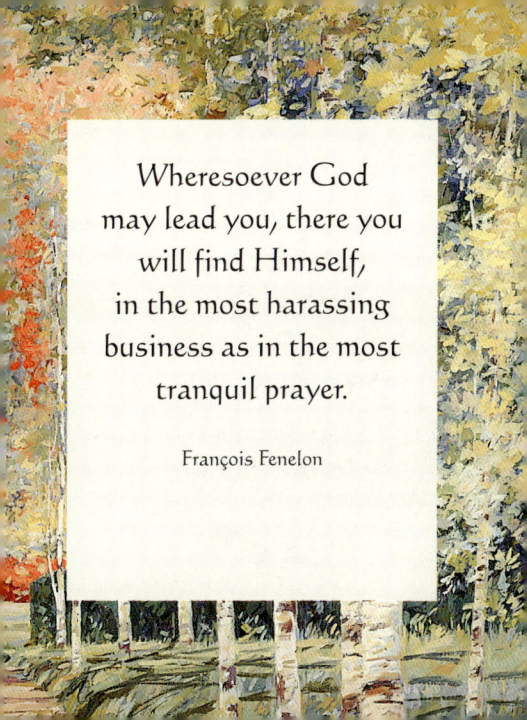

> Wheresoever God may lead you, there you will find Himself, in the most harassing business as in the most tranquil prayer.
>
> François Fenelon

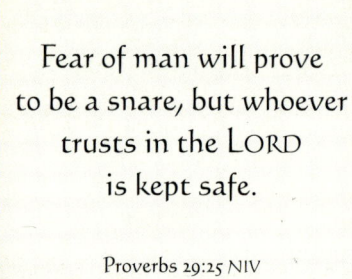

Fear of man will prove to be a snare, but whoever trusts in the LORD is kept safe.

Proverbs 29:25 NIV

Never did a believer in Jesus die or drown in his voyage to heaven.

Robert Traill

A greedy man stirs up dissension, but he who trusts in the LORD will prosper.

Proverbs 28:25 NIV

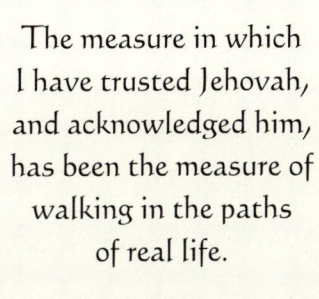

The measure in which
I have trusted Jehovah,
and acknowledged him,
has been the measure of
walking in the paths
of real life.

G. Campbell Morgan

Sweet are the uses of adversity, and this among them—that it brings into proper estimation mercies which were before lightly esteemed.

Charles Spurgeon

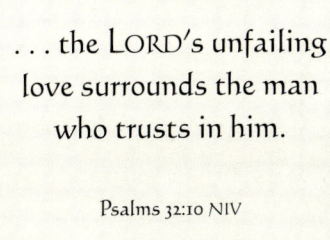

. . . the LORD's unfailing love surrounds the man who trusts in him.

Psalms 32:10 NIV

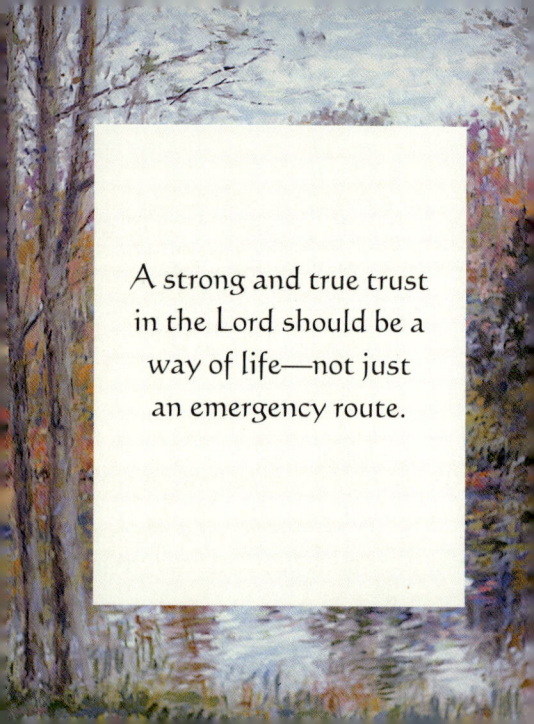

A strong and true trust in the Lord should be a way of life—not just an emergency route.

To you, O Lord, I lift up my soul; in you I trust, O my God.

Psalms 25:1-2 NIV

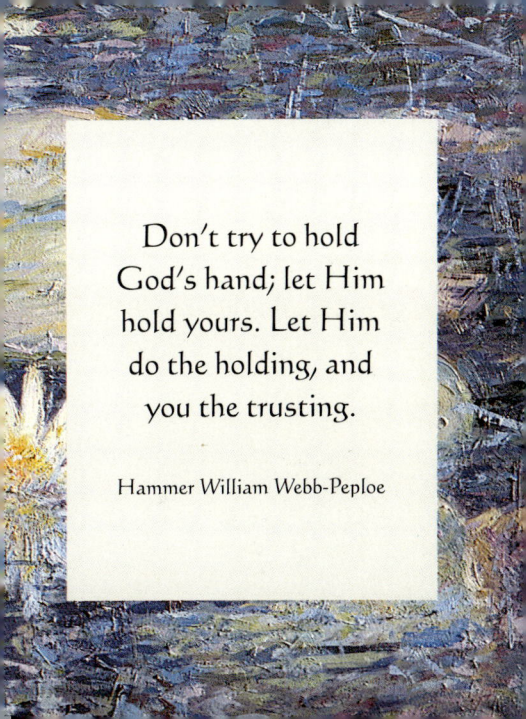

Don't try to hold God's hand; let Him hold yours. Let Him do the holding, and you the trusting.

Hammer William Webb-Peploe

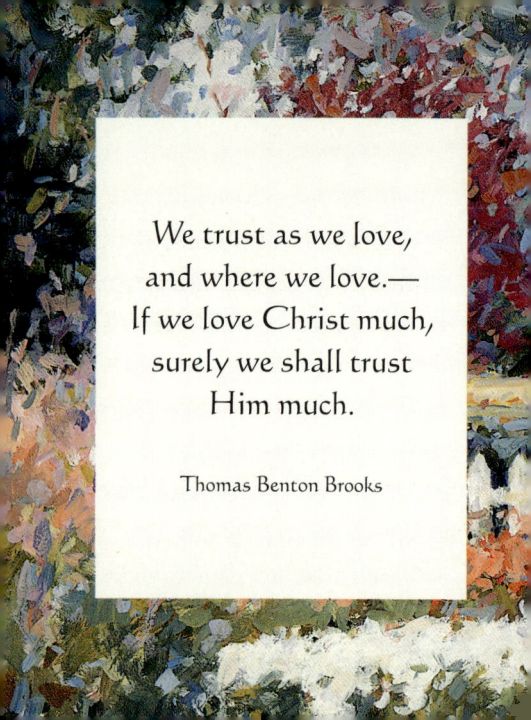

We trust as we love,
and where we love.—
If we love Christ much,
surely we shall trust
Him much.

Thomas Benton Brooks

O LORD of hosts,
how Blessed is the man
who trusts in Thee!

Psalms 84:12 NASB

A heart filled with trust looks up through the threatening storms to see the hand of God reaching down with love.

We cannot face the battles of life alone. We are strong only as we confront our problems together on our knees.

Valeene Hayes

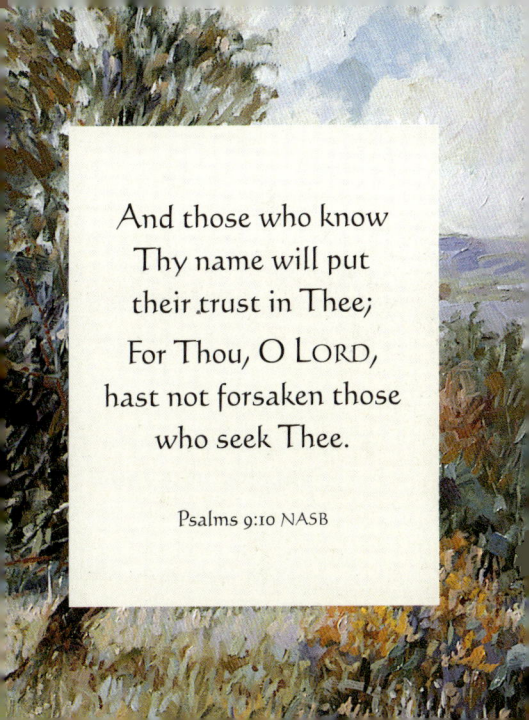

And those who know
Thy name will put
their trust in Thee;
For Thou, O Lord,
hast not forsaken those
who seek Thee.

Psalms 9:10 NASB

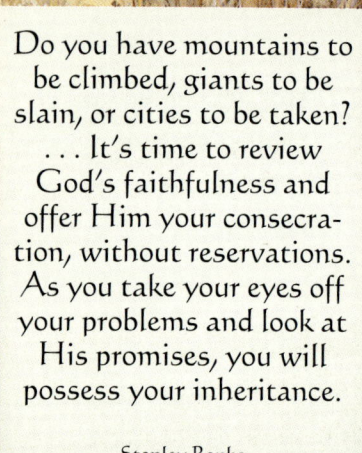

Do you have mountains to be climbed, giants to be slain, or cities to be taken? . . . It's time to review God's faithfulness and offer Him your consecration, without reservations. As you take your eyes off your problems and look at His promises, you will possess your inheritance.

Stanley Banks

In your unfailing love
you will lead the people
you have redeemed.
In your strength you
will guide them . . .

Exodus 15:13 NIV

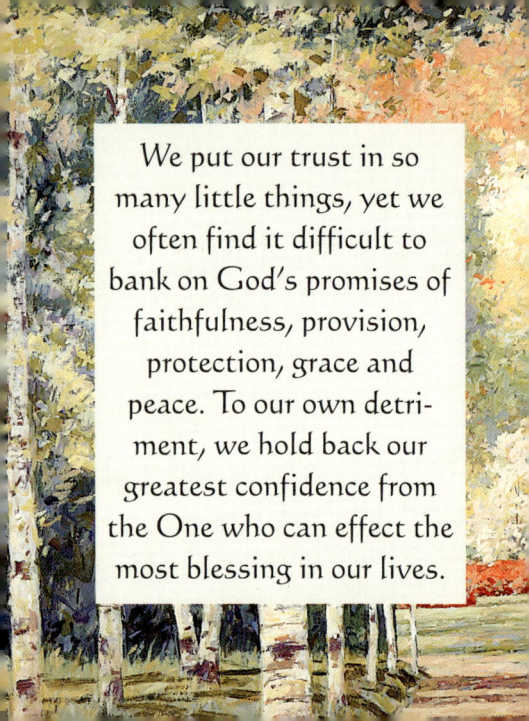

We put our trust in so many little things, yet we often find it difficult to bank on God's promises of faithfulness, provision, protection, grace and peace. To our own detriment, we hold back our greatest confidence from the One who can effect the most blessing in our lives.

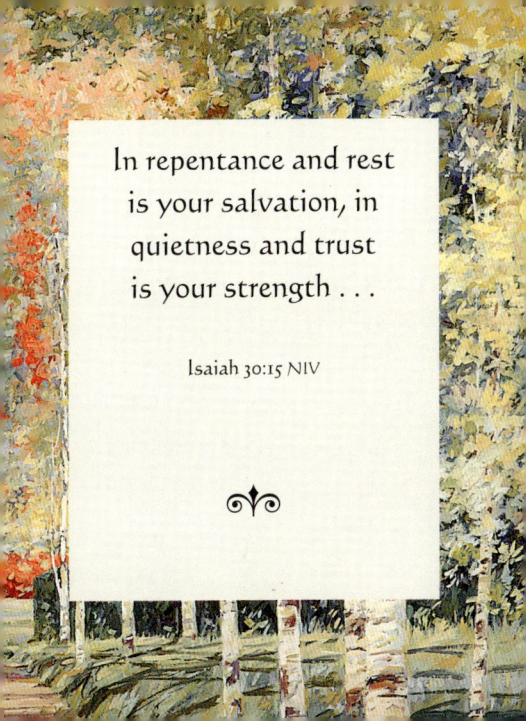

In repentance and rest
is your salvation, in
quietness and trust
is your strength . . .

Isaiah 30:15 NIV

Whether His providence is obscure or clear, it is always at work in your life—full of love, and right in the end. Remember that the tears of life belong to the interlude, not the finale, of your story.

Alice Huff

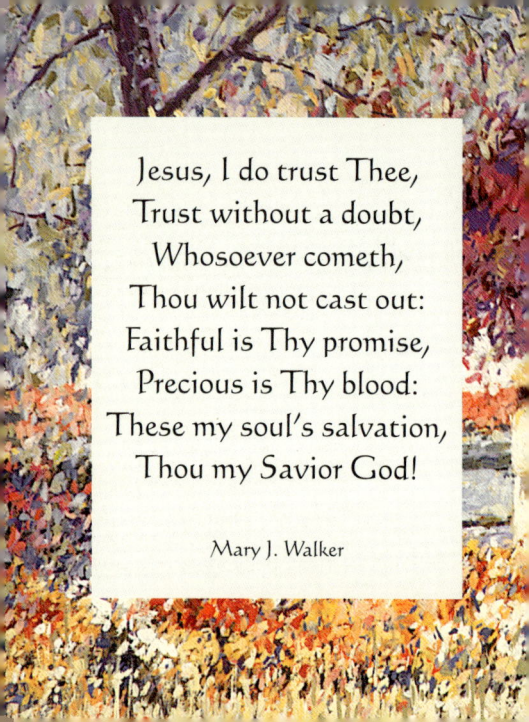

Jesus, I do trust Thee,
Trust without a doubt,
Whosoever cometh,
Thou wilt not cast out:
Faithful is Thy promise,
Precious is Thy blood:
These my soul's salvation,
Thou my Savior God!

Mary J. Walker

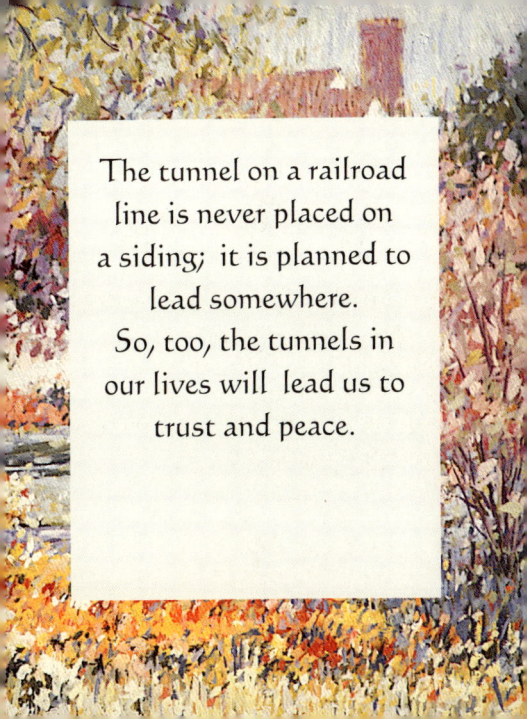

The tunnel on a railroad line is never placed on a siding; it is planned to lead somewhere.
So, too, the tunnels in our lives will lead us to trust and peace.

Our trust in the Lord is often enhanced by our remembering. Forgetting to remember brought the ancient Israelites to a point of doubt. The Israelites sent spies to Canaan and heard about the bounty within its borders. But they also heard about the giants.

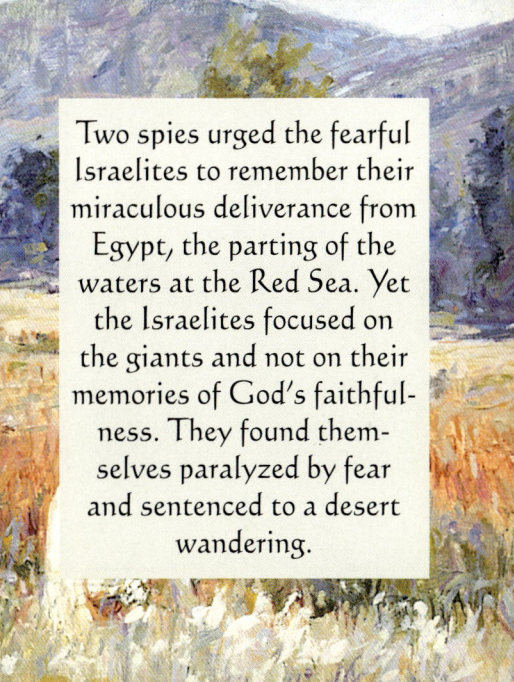

Two spies urged the fearful Israelites to remember their miraculous deliverance from Egypt, the parting of the waters at the Red Sea. Yet the Israelites focused on the giants and not on their memories of God's faithfulness. They found themselves paralyzed by fear and sentenced to a desert wandering.

Remember to remember. Remember God's trustworthiness as recorded in Scripture. Remember His faithfulness to you in the past. Remember, always remember. And then, when the giants cross *your* path, your focus will be on the Father's faithfulness, not on the fearful foe.

But blessed is the man who trusts in the LORD, whose confidence is in him. He will be like a tree planted by the water that sends out its roots by the stream. It does not fear when heat comes; its leaves are always green.

Jeremiah 17:7–8 NIV

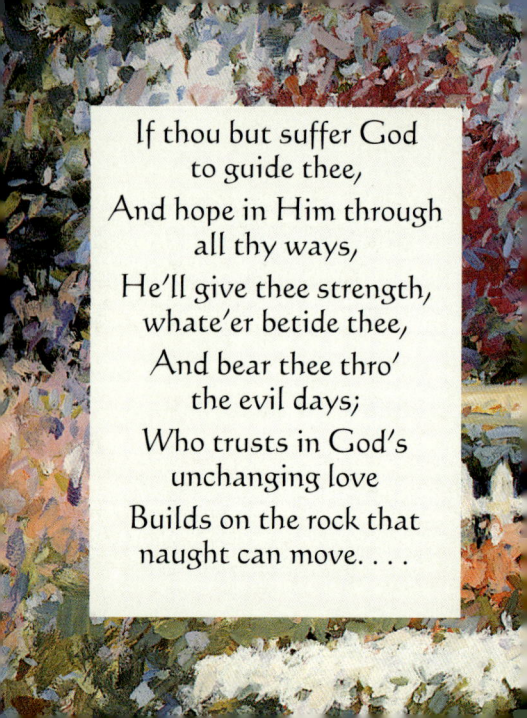

If thou but suffer God
to guide thee,
And hope in Him through
all thy ways,
He'll give thee strength,
whate'er betide thee,
And bear thee thro'
the evil days;
Who trusts in God's
unchanging love
Builds on the rock that
naught can move. . . .

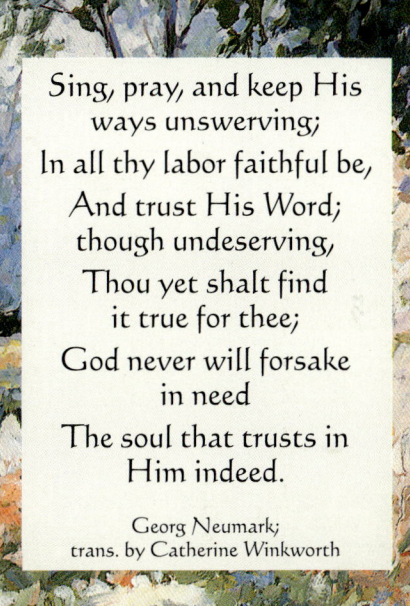

Sing, pray, and keep His ways unswerving;
In all thy labor faithful be,
And trust His Word; though undeserving,
Thou yet shalt find it true for thee;
God never will forsake in need
The soul that trusts in Him indeed.

Georg Neumark;
trans. by Catherine Winkworth

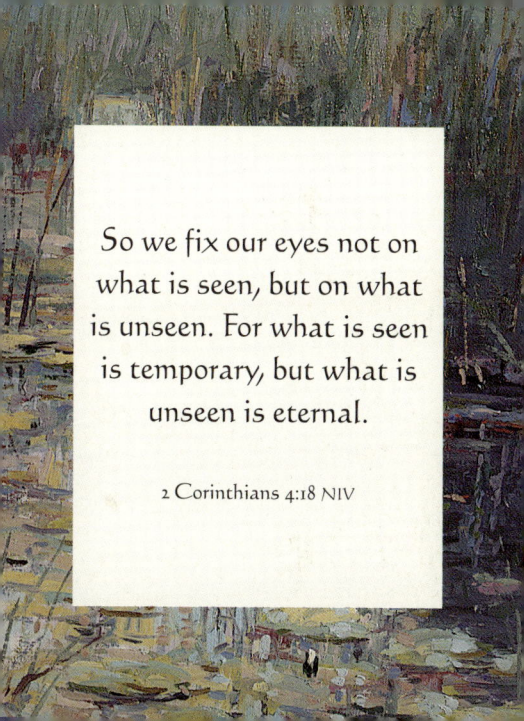

So we fix our eyes not on what is seen, but on what is unseen. For what is seen is temporary, but what is unseen is eternal.

2 Corinthians 4:18 NIV

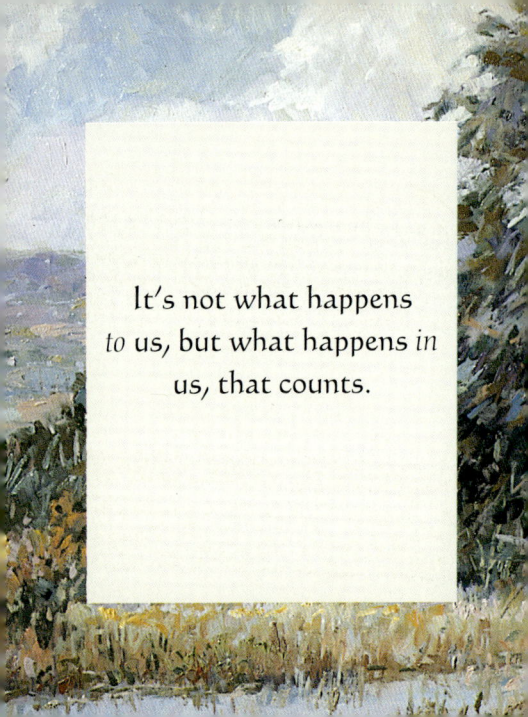

It's not what happens *to* us, but what happens *in* us, that counts.

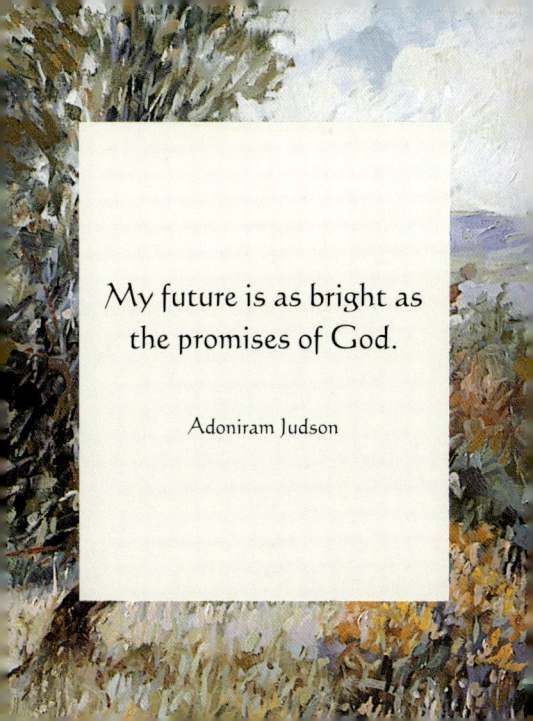

My future is as bright as the promises of God.

Adoniram Judson

Each of us may be sure that, if God sends us over rocky paths, He will provide us with sturdy shoes. He will never send us on any journey without equipping us well.

Alexander Maclaren

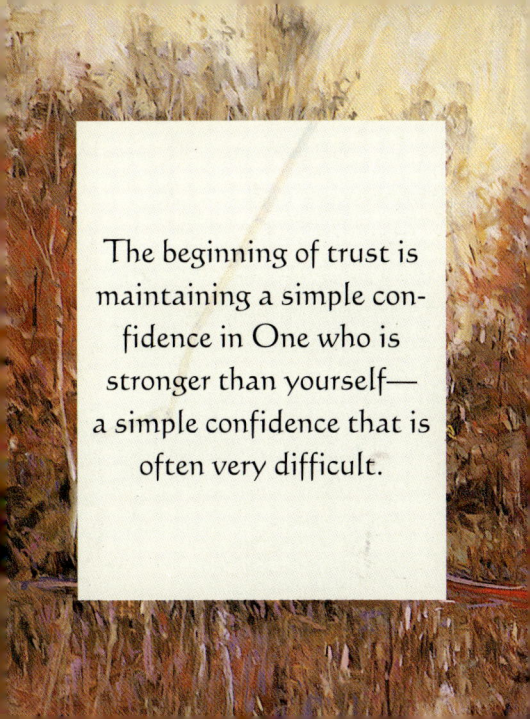

The beginning of trust is maintaining a simple confidence in One who is stronger than yourself—a simple confidence that is often very difficult.

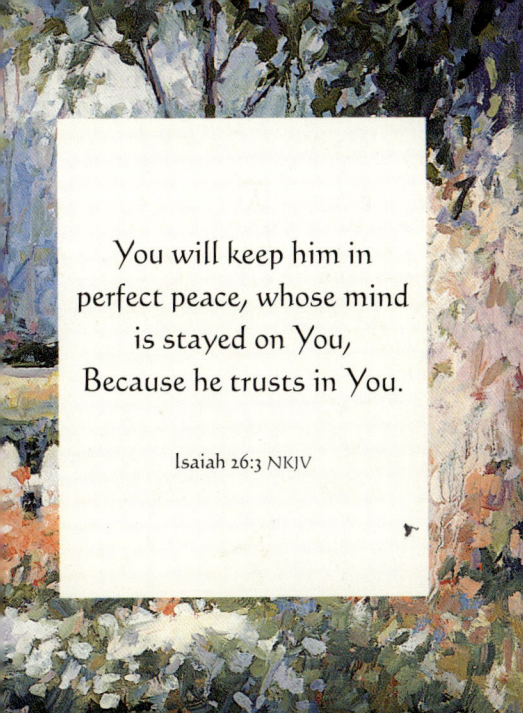

You will keep him in perfect peace, whose mind is stayed on You, Because he trusts in You.

Isaiah 26:3 NKJV

Our faith often lacks a childlike simplicity that is willing to trust the Lord when we cannot see what lies ahead. Restore, O Lord, a childlike faith to my heart!

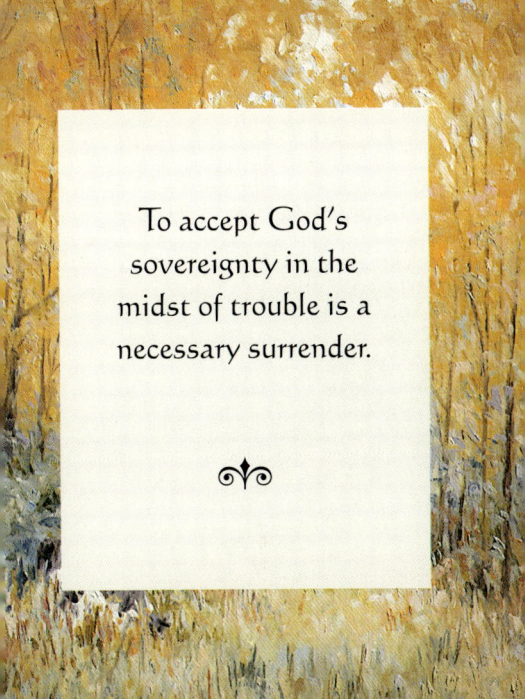

To accept God's sovereignty in the midst of trouble is a necessary surrender.

Commit your way to the LORD,

Trust also in Him, and He will do it.

Psalms 37:5 NASB

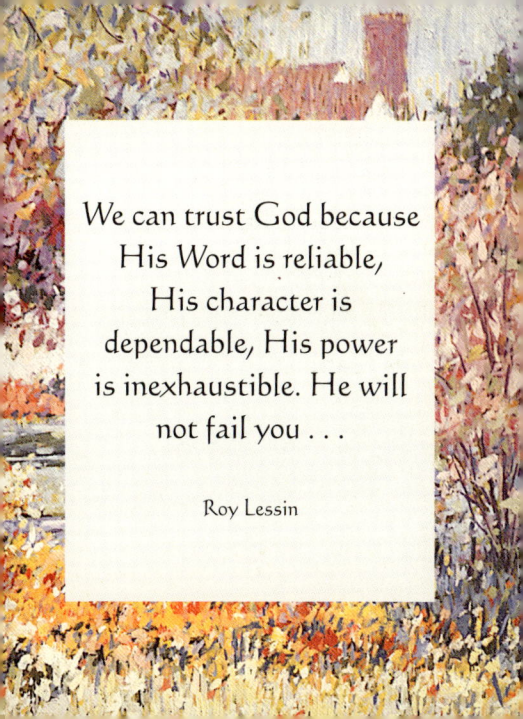

We can trust God because His Word is reliable, His character is dependable, His power is inexhaustible. He will not fail you . . .

Roy Lessin

Not a burden we bear,
not a sorrow we share,
But our toil He doth
richly repay;
Not a grief nor a loss,
not a frown nor a cross,
But is blest if we trust
and obey . . .
Trust and obey, for there's
no other way
To be happy in Jesus,
But to trust and obey.

John H. Sammis

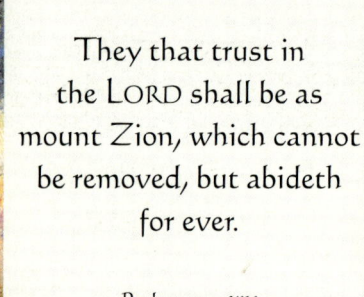

They that trust in the LORD shall be as mount Zion, which cannot be removed, but abideth for ever.

Psalms 125:1 KJV

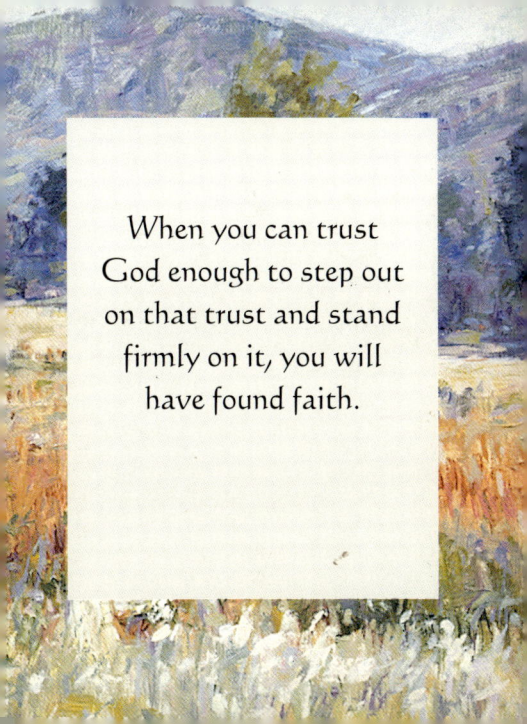

When you can trust God enough to step out on that trust and stand firmly on it, you will have found faith.

Be careful that you trust in God to provide; without trust you cannot obtain even the smallest of blessings.

Trust is hard earned,
and easily lost.

You who fear the LORD,
trust in the LORD;
He is their help and
their shield.

Psalms 115:11 NASB

If you but take one step
toward God

Though doubting makes
your vision dim

God will move toward
you a mile

And light your way
to Him.

If you think too much and fail to take action, fear makes its home within you.

Anonymous

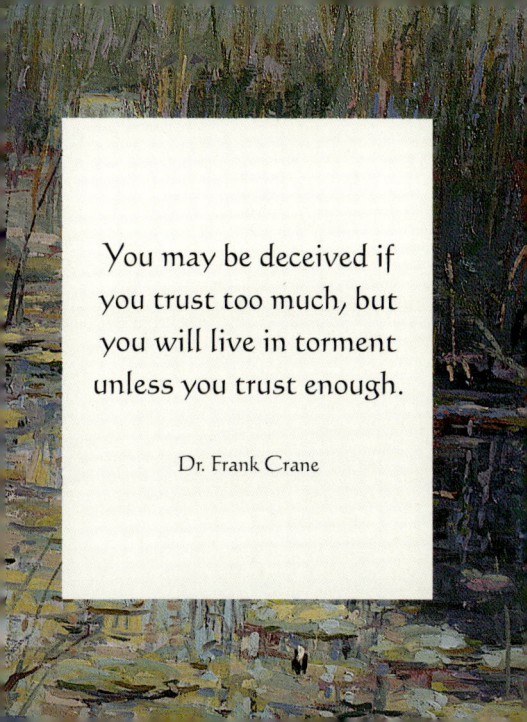

You may be deceived if you trust too much, but you will live in torment unless you trust enough.

Dr. Frank Crane

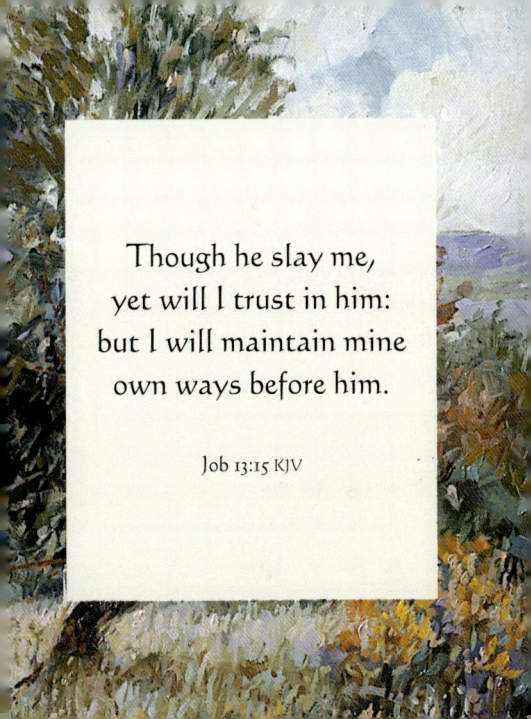

Though he slay me,
yet will I trust in him:
but I will maintain mine
own ways before him.

Job 13:15 KJV

No good work is ever done while the heart is hot and anxious and fretted.

Olive Schreiner

Some complain that God puts thorns on roses. Others trust God to help them find roses among the thorns.

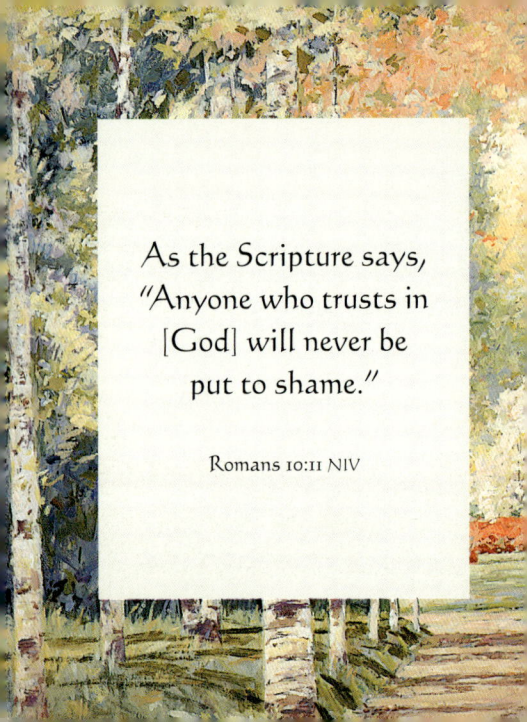

As the Scripture says, "Anyone who trusts in [God] will never be put to shame."

Romans 10:11 NIV

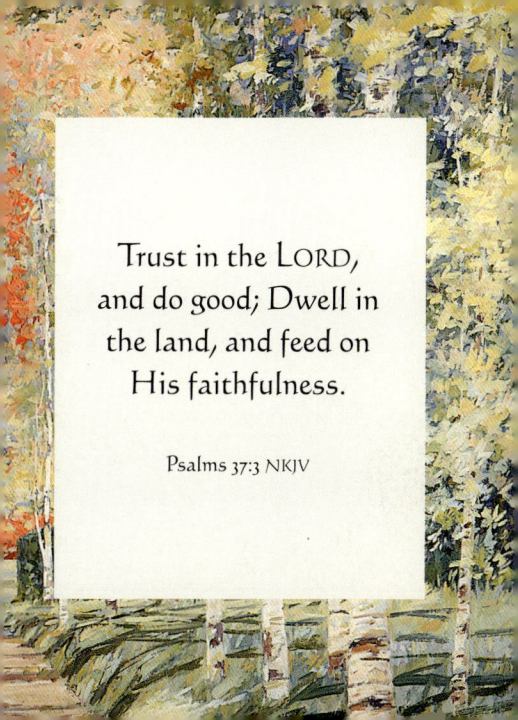

Trust in the LORD, and do good; Dwell in the land, and feed on His faithfulness.

Psalms 37:3 NKJV

Scripture quotations marked NKJV are taken from *The New King James Version* of the Bible. Copyright © 1979, 1980, 1982, 1994 by Thomas Nelson, Inc., Publishers. Used by permission.

Scripture quotations marked NASB are taken from the *New American Standard Bible*. Copyright © 1960, 1962, 1963, 1968, 1971, 1972, 1973, 1975, 1977 by The Lockman Foundation. Used by permission.

Scripture quotations marked NIV are taken from the *Holy Bible, New International Version*®. Copyright © 1973, 1978, 1984 by International Bible Society. Used by permission of Zondervan Publishing House. All rights reserved.

Scripture quotations marked KJV are taken from the *King James Version* of the Bible.